R O ⊕ T S

R O ⊙ T S

Advent and the Family Story of Jesus

DAN WILT

Printed in the United States of America

Cover and page design by Strange Last Name
Page layout by PerfecType, Nashville, Tennessee

Wilt, Dan.
  Roots : Advent and the family story of Jesus / Dan Wilt. –
Franklin, Tennessee : Seedbed Publishing, ©2022.

      pages ; cm. + 1 video disc

      ISBN: 9781628249774 (paperback)
      ISBN: 9781628249811 (DVD)
      ISBN: 9781628249781 (mobi)
      ISBN: 9781628249798 (epub)
      ISBN: 9781628249804 (pdf)
      OCLC: 1337492556

      1. Advent--Meditations. 2. Jesus Christ--Person and offices--Meditations.
      3. Jesus Christ--Genealogy--Meditations. 4. Devotional calendars.   I. Title.

BV40.W547 2022   242.33   2022943346

SEEDBED PUBLISHING
Franklin, Tennessee
seedbed.com

CONTENTS

AN INVITATION TO AWAKENING

This resource comes with an invitation.

The invitation is as simple as it is comprehensive. It is not an invitation to commit your life to this or that cause or to join an organization or to purchase another book. The invitation is this: to wake up to the life you always hoped was possible and the reason you were put on planet Earth.

It begins with following Jesus Christ. In case you are unaware, Jesus was born in the first century BCE into a poor family from Nazareth, a small village located in what is modern-day Israel. While his birth was associated with extraordinary phenomena, we know little about his childhood. At approximately thirty years of age, Jesus began a public mission of preaching, teaching, and healing throughout the region known as Galilee. His mission was characterized by miraculous signs and wonders; extravagant care of the poor and marginalized; and multiple unconventional claims about his own identity and purpose. In short, he claimed to be the incarnate Son of God with the mission and power to save people from sin, deliver them from death, and bring them into the now and eternal kingdom of God—on earth as it is in heaven.

In the spring of his thirty-third year, during the Jewish Passover celebration, Jesus was arrested by the religious authorities, put on trial in the middle of the night, and at their urging, sentenced to death by a Roman governor. On the day known to history as Good Friday, Jesus was crucified on a Roman cross. He was buried in a borrowed tomb. On the following Sunday, according to multiple eyewitness accounts, he was physically raised from the dead. He appeared to hundreds of people, taught his disciples, and prepared for what was to come.

Forty days after the resurrection, Jesus ascended bodily into the heavens where, according to the Bible, he sits at the right hand of God, as the Lord of heaven and earth. Ten days after his ascension, in a gathering of 120 people on the day of Pentecost, a Jewish day of celebration, something truly extraordinary happened. A loud and powerful wind swept over the people gathered. Pillars of what appeared to be fire descended upon the followers of Jesus. The Holy Spirit, the presence and power of God, filled the people, and the church was born. After this, the followers of Jesus went forth and began to do the very things Jesus did—preaching, teaching, and healing—planting churches and making disciples all over the world. Today, more than two thousand years later, the movement has reached us. This is the Great Awakening and it has never stopped.

Yes, two thousand years hence and more than two billion followers of Jesus later, this awakening movement of Jesus Christ and his church stands stronger than ever. Billions of ordinary people the world over have discovered in Jesus Christ an awakened life they never imagined possible. They have overcome challenges, defeated addictions, endured untenable hardships and suffering with unexplainable joy, and stared death in the face with the joyful confidence of eternal life. They have healed the sick, gathered the outcasts, embraced the oppressed, loved the poor, contended for justice, labored for peace, cared for the dying and, yes, even raised the dead.

We all face many challenges and problems. They are deeply personal, yet when joined together, they create enormous and complex chaos in the world, from our hearts to our homes to our churches and our cities. All of this chaos traces to two originating problems: sin and death. Sin, far beyond mere moral failure, describes the fundamental broken condition of every human being. Sin separates us from God and others, distorts and destroys our deepest identity as the image-bearers of God, and poses a fatal problem from which we cannot save ourselves. It results in an ever-diminishing quality of life and ultimately ends in eternal death. Because Jesus lived a life of sinless perfection, he is able to save us from sin and restore us to a right relationship with God, others, and ourselves. He did this through his sacrificial death on the cross on our behalf. Because Jesus rose from the dead, he is able to deliver us from death and bring us into a quality of life both eternal and unending.

This is the gospel of Jesus Christ: pardon from the penalty of sin, freedom from the power of sin, deliverance from the grip of death, and awakening to the supernatural empowerment of the Holy Spirit to live powerfully for the good of others and the glory of God. Jesus asks only that we acknowledge our broken selves as failed sinners, trust him as our Savior, and follow him as our Lord. Following Jesus does not mean an easy life; however, it does lead to a life of power and purpose, joy in the face of suffering, and profound, even world-changing, love for God and people.

All of this is admittedly a lot to take in. Remember, this is an invitation. Will you follow Jesus? Don't let the failings of his followers deter you. Come and see for yourself.

Here's a prayer to get you started:

> Our Father in heaven, it's me (say your name), I want to know you. I want to live an awakened life. I confess I am a sinner. I have failed myself, others, and you in many ways. I know you made me for a purpose and I want to fulfill that purpose with my one life. I want to follow Jesus Christ. Jesus, thank you for the gift of your life and death

and resurrection and ascension on my behalf. I want to walk in relationship with you as Savior and Lord. Would you lead me into the fullness and newness of life I was made for? I am ready to follow you. Come, Holy Spirit, and fill me with the love, power, and purposes of God. I pray these things by faith in the name of Jesus, amen.

It would be our privilege to help you get started and grow deeper in this awakened life of following Jesus. For some next steps and encouragements, visit seedbed.com/Awaken.

INTRODUCTION

When we think of Christmas, and the season of Advent that antici-pates it, many of us think of *family*. It is that strange mix of people we call mothers, fathers, sisters, brothers, cousins, aunts, uncles, grandparents, great grandparents, and even non-family members who aren't blood related to us (but feel as though they could be).

For us who follow Jesus, the body of Christ is also our family, and that bond we experience in this season provides us with more than just a spiritual lineage. It provides us with a new family, bonded by love and faith in the covenant-keeping God of the universe. It provides us with a sense of enduring connection to the people and land of Israel. It provides us a sense of our place in God's covenant story with humanity, weaving relentlessly through our personal and corporate histories—a story that reached its zenith in the life, death, resurrection, and ascension of our Lord Jesus.

Family.

Each family member has roots that we call a *family line*. Each family member has roots that we call our *family homeland*. Each family member has roots that we call our *heritage* or *family story*.

Jesus also has a family story. And that story is what this book is all about. The following words are from "Jesus Rises from the Root of Jesse," our first day's reflection in our Advent Journey:

> We all come from someone, somewhere, and something —a people, a place, and a story. We come from someone in our family line—parents, grandparents, great-grandparents, and so many others form extensions of the root system from which we each descend. We come

from somewhere, in that people are always physically located—we live in times and places unique to us, and even as we move from place to place we carry bits of our previous location with us in our hearts and memories. We come from something, in that we come from a story that is uniquely, remarkably, our own—while that story is also uniquely tied to our family line throughout history, and is ultimately tied to God's great love story with humanity.

To understand Jesus, we would do well to discover the root of faith from which he springs. It is a spiritual root system, in fact, that both Isaiah 11:1–3 and Matthew 1:1–17 are eager to convey.

Jesus, the Lord and Master of our lives, had roots that included a family line, a homeland, and a heritage or story. In his case, his family line could be traced all the way back to a leader like King David and, more specifically, his father, Jesse. The prophetic words of Isaiah point to Jesus' connection to Jesse, the father of David, and remind us just how important it was to the Hebrew people to understand the influences from the past that shaped one's life in the present.

A shoot will come up from the stump of Jesse; from his roots a Branch will bear fruit. The Spirit of the LORD will rest on him—the Spirit of wisdom and of understanding, the Spirit of counsel and of might, the Spirit of the knowledge and fear of the LORD—and he will delight in the fear of the LORD. (11:1–3)

Jesus not only had a family line that could be traced back to ancient times, but he also had a family homeland. The little strip of land we call Israel provided the ground Jesus walked on, yielded the fruits and foods he enjoyed, and hosted the towns and cities that dot the landscape of the Gospels and the New Testament. (I walked the streets of Bethlehem at night, many years ago, and found my imagination deeply stirred as I considered how, under those same skies so many revolutions of the sun ago, Jesus was born.)

Jesus not only had a family line and a family homeland; he also had a family story—a covenant heritage that brought together all the hopes and dreams of his people Israel into one, faith-bound narrative and guiding set of eternal truths. One need only to read through a few stories throughout the Scriptures to see that his people, the people of the covenant, are passionate, fallible, incredibly devoted, quick to tears, and as quick to laughter, hopeful yet capable of great despair, trusting yet capable of great disobedience, worshipful, yet capable of great idolatry.

Jesus himself carried those stories of his people, his place, and his story in his own heart. His life and ministry were absolutely, fundamentally built on the long, long story of humanity going back to Genesis.

Jesus has a family story, and Advent is the perfect time to explore it.

ENTERING ADVENT TOGETHER

When we as followers of Christ celebrate and worshipfully enter the seasons of Advent, Christmas, Epiphany, Lent, Easter, the Day of Ascension, and the Day of Pentecost, we are orienting our time—the currency of our lives—around the light and life of Jesus.

On a daily basis and with our calendars close at hand, we dutifully check our schedules day in and day out, conscientiously planning work and social events, making space for personal and family gatherings, and engaging thoughtfully with holidays and periods dedicated to honoring cultural voices or themes.

Yet followers of Jesus are invited, even welcomed, to orient our minutes, hours, days, and years in a sacred, intentional way. We can orient our schedules around what God has done to save the world, engaging with Christ-centered seasons designed to help us re-tell and re-enter the stories of the Gospels—year after year—allowing those stories to more deeply enter us.

Church history calls this way of ordering repeated annual seasons around Christ the Christian Year. We like to call it, in the work of Seedbed, the Awakening Calendar.

In his insightful book, *Ancient-Future Time: Forming Spirituality through the Christian Year*, the late Robert Webber said these words: "If we see the Christian year as an instrument through which we may be shaped by God's saving events in Christ, then it is not the Christian year that accomplishes our spiritual pilgrimage but Christ himself who is the very content and meaning of the Christian year."[1] Believers over millennia have found these words to ring true.

Advent is the beginning of the Christian New Year, the Awakening Calendar, and leads us into an entire new year of orientation to the fullness of God's work among us in the person of Jesus.

In celebrating Advent, Christ can meet us profoundly, as individuals and as communities, in dedicated seasons when we focus on an aspect, or an epic theme, of his world-loving story (John 3:16).

The journey we will take together this Advent, I trust and pray, will culminate in a deep joy for you on Christmas Day. Grace and peace to you as we enter Advent together—and as we explore the family story of Jesus.

---

1. Robert E. Webber, *Ancient Future Time: Forming Spirituality through the Christian Year* (Grand Rapids: Baker Books, 2004), 24.

JESUS RISES FROM THE ROOT OF JESSE

ISAIAH 11:1–3A

A shoot will come up from the stump of Jesse; from his roots a Branch will bear fruit. The Spirit of the LORD will rest on him—the Spirit of wisdom and of understanding, the Spirit of counsel and of might, the Spirit of the knowledge and fear of the LORD—and he will delight in the fear of the LORD.

CONSIDER THIS

We all come from someone, somewhere, and something—a people, a place, and a story. We come from someone in our family line—parents, grandparents, great-grandparents, and so many others form extensions of the root system from which we each descend. We come from somewhere, in that people are always physically located—we live in times and places unique to us, and even as we move from place to place we carry bits of our previous location with us in our hearts and memories. We come from something, in that we come from a story that is uniquely, remarkably, our own—while that story is also uniquely tied to our family line throughout history, and is ultimately tied to God's great love story with humanity.

It wouldn't be a stretch to say that you are not only made up of the breath of God in you and your own genetic configuration, you are also truly from the root of your family line that has gone before you. You are special, a branch from that root, if you will, and have been delivered to all of us as a gift of God's orchestration, the God who brings our paths to cross.

Entering into Advent, the season that inaugurates the Christian New Year, we open our spirits once again to the whole story of faith that Jesus came to reveal. Each Advent, we enter that story once again with deepened reverence, brimming worship, and expectant reflection on the person of Jesus. It is Jesus toward which the entirety of the biblical narrative points, from the Hebrew covenant to the new covenant, and in which we find the purposes of God acted out for our sake and for the sake of the world.

To understand Jesus, we would do well to discover the root of faith from which he springs. It is a spiritual root system, in fact, that both Isaiah 11:1–3 and Matthew 1:1–17 are eager to convey. The Son of God, it seems, the Lord's Messiah and our Ascended Master, did not come to us in a vacuum. He didn't descend from a strange, ethereal heaven in a mysterious cloud of divinity shimmering with an otherworldly glow. He came as a *child*, born naturally of a mother from a family line herself, and nurtured by a father who knew the names of his own kin many generations into the past. In Isaiah 11:1–3, that great prophetic passage that hails Christ's birth, we see that Jesus, the Branch, comes from the family line of the great King David, the son of Jesse, and from a long line of the faithful to which we point today saying, "Lord, as they said yes to you, so may we."

And it is here that we begin our Advent journey. The idea that has been traditionally known as a "Jesse Tree" will be our map. A Jesse Tree is an approach to the preparation season of Advent, leading us toward Christmas, that encourages us to revisit stories from the Hebrew Bible to help us understand the family line of Jesus and the spiritual mandate of the child born to save the world. We will draw from both Jesus' genealogical ancestry and his faith heritage, as we walk together on a journey through the stories of saints and sinners woven into the family line of the Son of God.

From a root, comes a branch. In that Branch—Jesus—you and I learn to abide in and draw from his unending resources (John 15:1–5), and in so doing, we are born again to eternal life. Let's begin.

THE PRAYER

Root of Jesse, the story you've woven together with our lives involves so many faithful men and women, people who lived and died, succeeded, stumbled, fell, got back up, and some who rose in faith to the call of their day. Open our hearts to learn from you as we step onto the path of your story, once again, this Advent season, a story into which you've woven us for your glory. We welcome you coming to us in a fresh and revelatory way this Advent. In Jesus' name, amen.

THE QUESTIONS

- Consider your own family line as far back as you have records, and those who sought to walk faithfully as well as those who stumbled and fell. Where can you see the gifts of God leading you to today, potentially those that came to you through your family?

- Consider your natural gifts, your appearance, your ways of thinking, and your location. Can you name a few gifts that came to you through your own family line?

JESUS SETS THE VISION OF NEW CREATION IN MOTION

GENESIS 1:26–27

Then God said, "Let us make mankind in our image, in our likeness, so that they may rule over the fish in the sea and the birds in the sky, over the livestock and all the wild animals, and over all the creatures that move along the ground."

So God created mankind in his own image, in the image of God he created them; male and female he created them.

CONSIDER THIS

Have you ever wished you could step back into a moment in time, in your history or the history of the world, to observe what actually took place? I have many of those moments on my list of "must visits," but only a few stand out and eclipse all the rest. This moment in time, sketched for us in words by Genesis 1:26–27, is one of those for me.

Humankind comes to life from the mud, the ground, of the earth. Breathed into being by the breath of the Mighty God, we walked in the garden of Eden as the vice-regents of creation. And as vice-regents, we were made to rule, lead, guide, steward, shepherd, and curate that creation—as God's emissaries on the earth.

When the Son of God comes into the world, he comes as one of us—as an image-bearer whose mandate is to steward the creation and shepherd it to its fruition—to become what we know as the new creation. Eden became both our imagined memory and our hopeful vision of the future; for Jesus, Eden was his actual memory (he was there at its creation) and his clear vision of the bright future of humankind.

And that memory, that vision, led him. It led him to serve. To give. To share. To teach. To clarify what being made of clay and divine breath actually means to a sojourner walking with God this side of heaven. To die as an offering for all, and to rise again as the first-born of all creation, Jesus set the vision in full, vibrant motion.

At the coming of God into the world, to take us by the hand and show us how human be-ing and be-coming is to be done, Jesus' life, death, and resurrection became the vehicle by which the Father took care of all manner of human business. As the "truly human" being, Jesus will show us the path to belovedness and to loving others through Jesus. He will show us the reason for our love of one another, our love of fruitful work, our love of children's laughter, and the taste of homemade bread. Jesus will show us the way to be human.

The early church father Bishop Irenaeus of Lyons said, "The glory of God is a human being, fully alive." Jesus will show us the way to live life to its very fullest, in the presence of the Father and in the presence of other image-bearers. Jesus will show us, in his Advent, the path from mud to glory. From him, we will learn to become who we were designed to be: God's breath in our lungs and God's light filling our hearts.

THE PRAYER

Emmanuel, today we are living in a story that did not begin with us, but sweeps us up in its narrative. We surrender again to being a beloved child who is here for a purpose, with a calling, with a destiny. Forgive us for seeing our lives as anything less than a mysterious miracle, and your life lived, given, and ushering in new creation life for us all as anything less than the story we now call our own. In Jesus' name, amen.

THE QUESTION

- It is fair to say that most of us forget that we are miracles, and that we often forget that central to Jesus' mission was to remind God's children of that fact. Using the word "miracle" in your sentence, how would you describe who you are and what the Father loves about you?

3

JESUS LOCATES US BEFORE THE FATHER

GENESIS 3:8–9

Then the man and his wife heard the sound of the LORD God
as he was walking in the garden in the cool of the day, and
they hid from the LORD God among the trees of the garden.
But the LORD God called to the man, "Where are you?"

CONSIDER THIS

The roots of Jesus, and for all of us, are watered by Eden's rain and fed by Eden's sunshine. We began in the presence of God, without fear, without rebellion, without shame, and without hatred.

Then, the first expressions of humankind, *adam* (meaning "ground" or "humankind"), used their will to make a choice that cut us off at the source, from the source, of our meaning. In that moment, as the fruit of the tree of the knowledge of good and evil was bitten into, bitten through—we became *lost*.

Lost. Lost is a term of meaning, of inner orientation, as well as being a term of location. When we are lost in our meaning, in orientation, we have lost our sense of purpose, our reference points, our context. In the garden, we lost our context—that we are all majestic creatures, rivaling anything in the celestial wonderland we call our universe, loved by the Creator who made us. We lost meaning. We welcomed in the chaos from which the world was formed, and it took residence in our disrupted, discontented hearts.

The Lord God called to the dust, to the ground, to the humans from the humus, "Where are you?" Our existential crisis, born from our sense of spiritual meaninglessness, had spun us around and left us wandering in the wasteland of our untamed desires.

When Jesus came into the world, he came as the answer to the Creator's question in the garden.

"Where are you?"

"Here, Father" said Jesus, *"Here we are, your humanity. Bring us back from exile; take us home."*

Jesus then became our Bridge and our Guide home, as one of us, and as the Lord of us, cutting paths through the thick weeds of pride and unforgiveness and self-hatred and self-sufficiency growing wild in our hearts. On the clear-cut ground our Leader has made before us, we learn to walk. Pulled to the left and the right again and again, "prone to wander," Lord, we feel it, "prone to leave the God" we love (from the hymn, "Come, Thou Fount"), Jesus comes to us this Advent to keep us on the path to life (Ps. 16:11).

There is no other way not to be lost—no other way than to be found by Jesus—and guided safely home.

Jesus, the Way to Life, you are here with us right now as we sit in your presence and lift our hands to you for guidance. We don't know the way home on our own; if you say "Where are you?" the best we can say in return is, "Here, Lord; find us, and take us home." Jesus, take us home. In Jesus' name, amen.

THE QUESTIONS

- We all wander in seasons of our lives. Can you think of a time in the past year when you were on the clear-cut path of life, but found yourself attracted back into the weeds once again? What reoriented you, reminded you, to stay on the path of life?

4

JESUS RENEWS BROKEN WORLDS THROUGH OBEDIENCE

GENESIS 6:7–8

So the LORD said, "I will wipe from the face of the earth the human race I have created—and with them the animals, the birds and the creatures that move along the ground—for I regret that I have made them." But Noah found favor in the eyes of the LORD.

CONSIDER THIS

Noah is one of the most fascinating characters we find in the extended family of Jesus. Noah walks a journey with his family that is remarkable both in its radiant faithfulness and its inescapable difficulty. When we think of Noah, we think of *obedience*. With just a dream and a schematic from God, Noah builds a massive boat that will float the animals of the world to safety as the land is reclaimed by an ocean of water—and reborn.

God's favor on Noah was a favor not built on talent, skill, or his parenting accomplishments. God's favor on Noah's life was built on Noah's steadfast commitment to see a great rescue through to the end. And that he did. The stories around that deliverance, written and unwritten, are every bit as important as the end result. But we know that God's goal was accomplished. An ark was built. Humanity and the created order of animals were saved. The rain came down, the waters rose, and Noah's ark was lifted toward heaven on the very floods of the world's judgment.

When Jesus entered the scene on that starry night in Bethlehem a few millennia ago, he did so as God's great spiritual ark, his very life and teaching designed to carry us to safety—into the harbor of the heart of the Father. And what do we see in Jesus' life that we see in Noah's life?

Obedience. Raw, Creator-trusting, crowd-defying, life-saving obedience.

Jesus was born, like us, not to do his own will, nor to see his own vision or purpose or meaning fulfilled and accomplished. Jesus was born to do the will of his Father, to move through the world as a sign that God speaks and guides the willing spirit that is humbly open to serving others.

From the manger where Mary and Joseph's obedience was put on display for all the world, Jesus would go on to learn the fullness of obedience through "what he suffered" (Heb. 5:8). So it is with us. We all have models of obedience in our lives, toward which we may look and remember each and every day. It is in the moments we face the choice between God's will being accomplished or our own—as Jesus experienced in the garden of Gethsemane—that our "your will be done" prayer leads us toward full maturity as a disciple of our Master.

Jesus, like Noah before him, chose obedience, and made himself a servant (Phil. 2:6–7). This Advent, following in their footsteps, so can we.

THE PRAYER

Obedient Lord, who stepped onto the soil of the human experience with love in your heart and a willing spirit, make us like you. In all the moments this season when we are faced with the choice to do our own will or yours, let us choose yours. In Jesus' name we pray, amen.

THE QUESTIONS

- Was there a time this past year when you faced just such a moment of obedience?

- Reading again about Noah's example, and considering Mary, Joseph, and Jesus leading by that same example, is there a situation impacting your life at the present in which you are beginning to sense what the Father's will is and the part you have to play? How will you respond?

5

JESUS KNOWS YOUR TRUE NAME

GENESIS 12:1–3

The Lord had said to Abram, "Go from your country, your people and your father's household to the land I will show you."

"I will make you into a great nation, and I will bless you; I will make your name great, and you will be a blessing. I will bless those who bless you, and whoever curses you I will curse; and all peoples on earth will be blessed through you."

CONSIDER THIS

The day you came into this world you had no name that came along with you. You and I were fresh from heaven, fresh from the hidden place of our nurture, brought into the wide-open world. We were an idea, a masterpiece, in the heart of God. We were born, we looked around, we took it all in (as far as we could see), and our little minds began to process all the information coming our way.

You were a *person*, with a set of genetics already in motion like billions of tiny gears within your system, processing the beautiful world before you. But you were, as far as human beings are concerned, *nameless*. The name given to you may have only been spoken before this moment in hushed tones by parents or family members, and perhaps you came into the world with just a few select individuals knowing your name. But the truth is, it's still the name they chose for you. We can trust in the sovereignty of God that our given names have come to us by some direction of divine care.

But there is a name that God has for you and for me, known to him and to be known fully by us one day.[2] The process of life is to discover God's name for you, for me, and for that identity to emerge more and more beautifully until the day we see him face-to-face!

Abram had a name. Then, at a key point in his journey, God changed it. He went from "exalted father" to "father of a multitude." Abram could embrace being an exalted father. He had some evidence that he was a highly honored father in his life. But "father of a multitude"? That took some faith to swallow. That name came from God. Eventually, Abraham must have gone from saying his new name with a question mark every time he looked in the mirror at his aging face, to saying his new name with a bold confidence that can only come from a wild faith in an untameable God.

Jesus, like Abraham, lived into the name the Father gave him. Y'shua, "The Lord Saves," was what he would hear every time his mother called him for dinner. Hebrew is a verb-based language, and the action of the Lord "saving" would become the action that would mark every aspect of Jesus' life.

Emerging victorious from the grave, Jesus, like the Father, names us with names that feel beyond our scope of understanding. To Jesus, we are "Beloved," and "Body," and "Saints," and so much more. To Jesus, you are "Loved," "Friend," "Blessed," "Redeemed," "Strong," "Free," and so much more.

---

2. See Revelation 2:17; see also N. T. Wright's *Revelation for Everyone*.

The Lord who comes to us all in Advent is coming to you to affirm your name, known to him. Live into it by living into some of the names listed. As you do, you'll become more fully the one Jesus names his very own.

THE PRAYER

Naming God, who calls things that are not as though they are, and who calls us according to who you know us to be, show us who we are in your sight. Open our hearts to receive your love, and your affirmation, that we may be free to become a sign of your great presence in the world. Our names are in your hands, and we are ready for you to call us to your vision of greatness. In Jesus' name, amen.

THE QUESTIONS

- Have you ever thought about the fact that God has a name for you that is written on his heart, and that he is calling you to fulfill? What characteristics about you do you think are expressed in God's hidden name for you?

6

JESUS AND HIS FAMILY LAUGH

GENESIS 21:1–3, 6–7

Now the LORD was gracious to Sarah as he had said, and the LORD did for Sarah what he had promised. Sarah became pregnant and bore a son to Abraham in his old age, at the very time God had promised him. Abraham gave the name Isaac to the son Sarah bore him. . . .

Sarah said, "God has brought me laughter, and everyone who hears about this will laugh with me." And she added, "Who would have said to Abraham that Sarah would nurse children? Yet I have borne him a son in his old age."

CONSIDER THIS

Sarah *laughed,* and I get it. What she heard the Lord say was pure, unadulterated, *funny.* I've heard the Lord speak things to me that I thought were funny at the time. God has a knack for the practical joke that's not actually a joke, for stand-up comedy that is a call to stand up and has comedic yet powerful timing and results.

Jesus comes from a long line of people who *laugh.* He comes from a people who praise loudly, and who lament the same; from a people who laugh hard and who cry even harder. More than this, Jesus comes from a people who are honest to God, who pull no punches, and who wrestle with him until their hip is out of joint and they have received his blessing.

Before Sarah laughed in Genesis 18:9–15, Abraham fell down on his face and laughed first in 17:17. We can laugh in bewilderment and thanks, or we can laugh in derision and mockery. We'll never know exactly how Sarah laughed or Abraham laughed, but it seems the Lord was not offended by it. They were not rebuked; they just had to be honest about how they really felt.

At the Advent of the Incarnate One, we can only imagine the shepherds laughing with joy after the angels make their announcement. We can almost hear Mary and Joseph laugh in the manger, that smiling laugh so common to a mother and father when they first hold a newborn in their arms. And as far as we know, Jesus may have laughed at his own jokes and even, perhaps, the jokes of others (sometimes laughing at another's joke is an act of godly compassion, as we all know!).

Would it honor the Lord for you to laugh with joy, with thanks, with others this Advent season? The Lord of Laughter may lead you to it; his desire being that you throw off the heavy weights of the last year and delight in just how faithful he has shown himself to be.

Laughter is not only the best medicine; sometimes it is also the best prayer.

THE PRAYER

Lord of Laughter, we would like to experience delight again in all you are doing in us and around us. Where the spirit of heaviness has us bound, let the oil of joy (Isa. 61:3) lift it off of us as we bless you for the precious gifts you are giving us in this new season of delight.

- How long has it been since you laughed, really hard, with friends, family, or before God?

- What could you do to put your heart in such a posture as to be willing to express joy in a new and unbridled way as the Christian New Year begins?

7

JESUS IS THE PROVISION ON THE MOUNTAIN

GENESIS 22:1–2, 13–14

Some time later God tested Abraham. He said to him, "Abraham!"

"Here I am," he replied.

Then God said, "Take your son, your only son, whom you love— Isaac—and go to the region of Moriah. Sacrifice him there as a burnt offering on a mountain I will show you." . . .

Abraham looked up and there in a thicket he saw a ram caught by its horns. He went over and took the ram and sacrificed it as a burnt offering instead of his son. So Abraham called that place The LORD Will Provide. And to this day it is said, "On the mountain of the LORD it will be provided."

CONSIDER THIS

Christmas celebrations surrounding the birth of Jesus are often fueled by pleasant reminiscences and nostalgia. We may hear the sounds of carols we heard from our youth ringing in malls and shops. We may smell the fragrance of a grandma's candles, scented with the season. We may feel soft evergreen needles on our palms as we purchase this year's Christmas tree. All of these moments can trigger memories that go back as far as we can remember.

But a deeper remembering, a holy *anamnesis*, could take us back to sights, sounds, and smells less appealing to our holiday sensibilities. We might return to Mount Moriah, to the sound of a father wailing as he prepared to sacrifice his only son, the smell of altar wood on a mountain smoking to life, the feeling of a blade sitting heavy in the hand, and the cool touch of a ram's horn as it is drawn from a thicket.

The LORD Will Provide.

From the ancestral family of Jesus is a plot line that always moves forward through stories of great risk, great courage, and great acts of faith—acts that have changed the course of your life and mine. Abraham preparing to sacrifice Isaac on the mountain is just one stop on that plot line—but it's an important one. Whispers of a promised provision make little sense when your son is bound to an altar and you have been asked to take the greatest leap of faith/fear you've ever known. Pausing on Mount Moriah, we meet Jesus as the provision of God.

The LORD Will Provide.

When Christ picked up his cross to walk the long road to Golgotha, the overtones ringing across the millennia would have been unmissable by those who had begun to understand his teaching. Jesus did not resist the Father's request any more than Abraham did. He opened himself to the possibility that there would be no redemption that followed his great act of sacrifice, of faith, but knew that he must take the step no matter what. His obedience would lead somewhere, we know—but how could Jesus truly be assured that all things would work together for the good in that moment of decision?

Jesus is the descendant of the obedient-soul, the hearing-and-obeying saint, the Lord-I-am-your-servant bloodline of Abraham, David, Mary, and others. The family line of Jesus obeys the voice

DAN WILT

of the Lord and trusts in him to be the provision we need. You and I are now a part of that line.

It's here we discover that Jesus would not only sacrifice himself for the sake of the world as our incarnate Messiah, he would also call us to pour out our lives on behalf of others in the same, complete, fully expended way.

The LORD Will Provide.

Jesus is the Provision of God for the sacrifice, the redemption, the healing of the human heart; you and I are the living sacrifices that carry the news of that provision to the ends of the earth.

THE PRAYER

Lord Who Provides, your acts of care and provision startle us. We may never be fully confident you will act when you say you will, but make us always willing to take the leap of faith that leads to your life and ways being highlighted in this world. Use us to glorify you in celebration or sacrifice; and let us be a living sacrifice to you—carrying the message of your provision of love into the world you have put in front of us. In Jesus' name, amen.

THE QUESTIONS

- How has living a sacrificial life helped you to understand the act of Jesus giving himself for the world?

- With what do you most identify about his suffering and self-offering to the world?

8

JESUS IS LORD OF THE WRESTLING HEART

GENESIS 32:22–24, 28

That night Jacob got up and took his two wives, his two female servants and his eleven sons and crossed the ford of the Jabbok. After he had sent them across the stream, he sent over all his possessions. So Jacob was left alone, and a man wrestled with him till daybreak. . . .

Then the man said, "Your name will no longer be Jacob, but Israel, because you have struggled with God and with humans and have overcome."

CONSIDER THIS

Our Advent reflection on the roots of Jesus' family tree takes us back to the moment in time when his forefather Jacob was first called "Israel"—and an entire people would bear his name for all recorded history.

When I was a young boy, at the prodding of a few friends, I tried the sport of wrestling. Two people get in a ring and attempt to force the other to physically submit. If there is one word that captures what happens in the ring, it is *resistance*; the entire sport is built on two people applying resistance, pressure, force to the other. When one person is pinned to the ground, the bell rings and the match is over. I was pinned often, but I did learn to apply my strength, like Jacob, in the process.

Jacob is mentioned, along with his grandfather, Abraham, and his father, Isaac, in Jesus' genealogy in Matthew 1:2. Jacob was, by all accounts, a *wrestler*, a *resistor*, a *pressurer*, a *forcer*—always to get his own way. He was a man in a *struggle* his entire life. He wrestled with his brother coming out of the womb, and he wrestled a birthright and a blessing from him as well. Jacob psychologically wrestled his father out of a gift that was not intended for him, and he wrestled with his father-in-law over issues of fairness. Jacob knew how to get his way.

Deception. Resistance. Impatience. Struggle. Do these sound like words you would expect to be associated with a man who would not only become the namesake of the myriad people of Abraham, but would also make it into the genealogy of the Messiah? We can all be thankful that the Son of God has broken people who are a part of his family. Sometimes what we overcome is the very sign and signal that God is with us, working all things for the good for those who love him and are called according to his purposes (Rom. 8:28). In overcoming, we become ensigns of grace.

But why did Jacob struggle, and why do we? Jacob's greatest opponent, as we read at various points in his story (see Gen. 31:1; 32:7, 11) was *fear*. At the ford of the Jabbok, Jacob sends his family, herds, and flocks ahead of him. Alone with his fear of facing his brother Esau, he spends the night in a wrestling match with a figure he seems to understand to be God. Jacob will name the place Peniel, which means "face of God," because he saw God face-to-face, and yet his life was spared (Gen. 32:30). When the close-quarters, life-transforming match is over, Jacob is given the new name, *Israel*—one who "struggles" with God.

The only remedy for fear, according to 1 John 4:18, is love. Jacob feared because, like us, he struggled with love. He must have found it hard to love himself knowing all he had done. He must have found it hard to love others because he felt so unloved and unfavored himself. That's how *takers* are born. They are always looking to provide something for themselves that only God can give. That night, perhaps, just perhaps, Jacob was ultimately overcome by love—humbled by love. And having met with God in the midst of his deepest fear, overpowering love left him with a limp of humility as a memento of the experience.

Jesus wrestled in a garden called Gethsemane. He, however, knew he was beloved, and could freely love because of that inner solidity and contentment. Our Messiah, knowing in his own family line how fear can corrupt and disorient a soul, steps into our lives and says, as he did to the disciples, "Don't be afraid" (Matt. 14:27). With those words we are welcomed to lay down our resistance, our impatience, our hiding in shame, our deception, our *wrestling*—to embrace the beloved, loving, brave life of Jesus.

THE PRAYER

Lord of the Humbled Heart, you know us, and you always have. May our fear be broken by your love, casting it out, day by day, from our hearts. Give us the humility that comes from having been overcome by love, and we'll take any limp that comes with it to remind me of love's strength for the journey. In Jesus' name, amen.

THE QUESTIONS

- How has the love of Jesus met you in your fear and dissolved its power in your life?

- Are there areas of fear you are holding onto that you could surrender to Jesus without resistance?

9

JESUS BRINGS GOOD FROM EVIL

GENESIS 50:19–20

But Joseph said to them, "Don't be afraid. Am I in the place of God? You intended to harm me, but God intended it for good to accomplish what is now being done, the saving of many lives."

CONSIDER THIS

As we continue our journey through Advent and its themes of hope, love, joy, and peace, why are we spending so much time in Genesis? The Lord Jesus who appears to us in his Advent, at the fullness of time (Gal. 4:4–7), is a branch from a family tree that shoots its strong roots deep into the soil of the earliest recorded human history. Jesus' family tree and family story have withstood the most violent spiritual weather events of the ages. The gates of hell will simply not prevail against the church, whose story is now a part of the story of Christ (Matt. 16:17–19).

Joseph is an important figure in the faith root system of Jesus and of each one of us today. From his humble beginnings, to his technicolor dream coat, to his slavery and imprisonment, to his revelatory gifts, to his remarkable ascent to political power, to his commanding presence as the vizier of the great Pharaoh, Joseph's story of faith reveals many profound truths that can keep us on the path to life (Ps. 16:11).

In Genesis 50:19–20, when Joseph finally reveals himself to his betraying brothers, he uses these halting words: "You intended to harm me, but God intended it for good." Though Joseph's path was treacherous and life-threatening, it led him to a place where he could save his people, along with the Egyptians, during the bleak years of a widespread famine.

Jesus, Master of the human heart and Great Deliverer from the bondage of sin, was done tremendous harm on his journey. The story of the life of Joseph must have sprung to mind often in early church gatherings, having seen their Lord unjustly treated at the hands of the empire and even a close friend, and then rising as the ascended Lord before their very eyes!

Yet, as Jesus walked his own harrowing journey in his first Advent coming, the Father had a purpose pulsing behind it all. With the name *Jesus* ("the Lord saves") guiding and framing his mission, Jesus' path led him to the place where he could intervene to save every single one of us who trust in his name. Like Joseph before him, all that the enemy intended for evil in Jesus' life was turned to *good*.

We know the stories that followed Jesus' triumph, because they are our own. Evil manifests itself in many lives in many different ways, and our enemy intends to steal, kill, and destroy each one of us. That's the enemy's plan, and it's on the agenda every day. But what does Jesus do? He *intervenes*.

He takes all that evil and pain and suffering and hopelessness in our lives and "works for the good of those who love him, who have been called according to his purpose" (Rom. 8:28). You and I are living examples that Jesus brings good from evil. Pause here to worship with me! Our Advent Lord turns evil to good! The enemy has no cards left in his hand for all eternity!

This Advent, Jesus is at work for your good and mine. You need not be enslaved to the power of evil or its effects anymore, nor does fear have the authority to command your daily thoughts, emotions, and actions unless you give it that place of authority. Today you can celebrate that you are beloved, you are a cared-for soul, and God is working all things for your good—to his glory.

THE PRAYER

Lord of the Great Conversion, we thank you that you are always converting the hard stories in our lives into radiant testimonies of your faithfulness. This Advent, we defer and surrender to your work in the midst of the challenges we are facing. We revel in your promise to "make everything new" (Rev. 21:5) when you come again in all your glory. In Jesus' name, amen.

THE QUESTIONS

- Is there a hard story in your life that Jesus turned for good, that is now a beautiful and important part of your testimony of God's faithfulness?

- Like Joseph, how has God used that story to impact the lives of others around you?

10

JESUS IS THE LAMB OF GOD

EXODUS 12:24–28

"Obey these instructions as a lasting ordinance for you and your descendants. When you enter the land that the LORD will give you as he promised, observe this ceremony. And when your children ask you, 'What does this ceremony mean to you?' then tell them, 'It is the Passover sacrifice to the LORD, who passed over the houses of the Israelites in Egypt and spared our homes when he struck down the Egyptians.'" Then the people bowed down and worshiped. The Israelites did just what the LORD commanded Moses and Aaron.

CONSIDER THIS

The Advent roots of Jesus' story and the roots of the faith-family of Israel—as well as the roots of the body of Christ of which we are a part—are nourished by a few striking images from the Old Testament. One of these images is the picture of the sacrificial lamb, sacrificed for the sins of the people of Israel. While we won't unpack such a powerful and complex image completely, it's important that we take a few moments this Advent season to reflect on Jesus coming into the world as the *Agnus Dei*—the Lamb of God.

In the Scriptures, we hear Christ called the "Lamb of God who takes away the sins of the world" (John 1:29). In the ancient Hebrew image of the sacrificial lamb, the Jews would sacrifice a lamb in the Passover celebration, as a life-for-life offering that would cleanse the sin of the nation and remind them of God's great, life-saving deliverance of his people from the Egyptians. That sacrifice would cleanse the guilt and sin of the people of Israel as they stumbled to uphold their end of covenant obedience and loving-kindness intended to be shared between themselves and God.

While an image like a sacrificial lamb can feel offensive to our modern sensibilities, it is important that we approach images like this with tremendous historical *humility*—we are not better or smarter than they are—they lived in a time and in a place, in a world that would be very unfamiliar to us today. God speaks in history, in time, to people in ways that are meaningful to them, using powerful images like a sacrificial lamb to show us just how far God will go to win us back, heal us from our sin, and keep us aware that we are in need of a savior who will offer his life in exchange for our own.

Advent is the Father's action to restore the covenant relationship, broken in the garden of Eden, between God and humanity, between us and our Creator. By giving his one and only Son to live, die, and rise to life again among us, the Father was bridging the gap between himself and us, a gap created by our sin and widened through our endless rebellion and misuse of the precious gifts of creation—including one another.

At Christmas, Christ came to us as the Lamb of God. On the cross, he would make the supreme sacrifice for you, for me, for all of the human family. When Jesus was born, one of the gifts given to him by one of the Gentile kings was myrrh, a spice with many uses, one of which was its use as a burial spice (Matt. 2:11; John 19:39).

Myrrh is mentioned a few times in Jesus' story, foreshadowing that he will give his life, as a sacrificial lamb (Rev. 13:8), as a ransom for us all (Mark 10:45). As the song says, "Mary, did you know?" Did you know that Jesus was born to die for us all?

First Peter 1:18–20 says: "For you know that it was not with perishable things such as silver or gold that you were redeemed from the empty way of life handed down to you from your ancestors, but with the precious blood of Christ, a lamb without blemish or defect. He was chosen before the creation of the world, but was revealed in these last times for your sake." The Lamb of God was slain for us, a sacrifice that forever breaks the power of sin, brings forgiveness, and triumphs over the powers and authorities of this cruel world, making a spectacle of them on the cross where the Lamb of God suffered and died (Col. 2:13–15).

Advent reminds us that Jesus is, and will always be, the Lamb of God who takes away the sin of the world. We will worship him as the Lamb, forever (Rev. 5:12–13).

THE PRAYER

Lamb of God, you take away the sin of the world—and our own right along with it. We rise today, clean and cleansed in spirit and conscience, brought into sweet intimacy with you, because you took our sin on your shoulders in your death, and rose to defeat its power forever. Thank you. We worship you, Lamb of God, in this season of Advent. In Jesus' name, amen.

- Have you ever meditated on Jesus as the Lamb of God during the Advent season? If not, take some time to reflect on what it means for Jesus to be the "Lamb of God who takes away the sins of the world" and how his sacrifice for you has changed your life.

11

JESUS IS THE WORD MADE FLESH

JOHN 1:1, 14

In the beginning was the Word, and the Word was
with God, and the Word was God. . . .

The Word became flesh and made his dwelling among us.
We have seen his glory, the glory of the one and only Son,
who came from the Father, full of grace and truth.

CONSIDER THIS

As we move through Advent and rediscover the roots of Jesus, we note once again that he came to us from a people, a place, and a story. A second, powerful image that runs through the story of Jesus, weaving through the Old Testament and culminating in the New Testament, is the image of Christ as the Word of God made flesh (John 1:14).

In Advent we prepare our hearts to receive the message anew that Jesus was born in Bethlehem as the Word of God among us— the living Word of God. Jesus moved and communicated as the embodiment, the very expression, of the heart of God. That's what words do, and that's what Jesus did as the Word of God made flesh.

For the ancient Hebrews, words held great meaning and power. While we are often flippant about our use of words today, the Jews understood that God, by his Word, spoke the entire cosmos into being (Gen. 1:3). The decrees and laws spoken through Moses held power for keeping Israel in alignment with the character of God and the goodness of his covenant. In fact, the people needed Moses to do the talking for God because they were afraid to have God speak to them for fear they would die (Ex. 20:1–19). God's Word holds power (Prov. 18:21; James 3), and when the first cries emerged from the rough stable in the Christmas story, that power was resident in Jesus.

Jesus is God's speech to us. In the Bible, God's speech is always creative, healing, penetrating, and transforming. Jesus is God's Word to you, to me, and to humanity. God's Word to us, in Christ, is creative, healing, penetrating, and transforming. In other words, God's Word, Jesus, is *life*.

Hebrews 1:1–3a says this about the baby born in Bethlehem:

> In the past God spoke to our ancestors through the prophets at many times and in various ways, but in these last days he has spoken to us by his Son, whom he appointed heir of all things, and through whom also he made the universe. The Son is the radiance of God's glory and the exact representation of his being, sustaining all things by his powerful word.

In Advent we revel in the reality that "The Word became flesh and made his dwelling among us. We have seen his glory, the glory of the one and only Son, who came from the Father, full of grace and truth" (John 1:14).

When we feel as though we can't hear the voice of God, we can simply open our Bibles to the Gospels and watch God's speech in full, powerful motion! The life of Jesus is God speaking to us; we can hear his words knowing that we are hearing the very words of God.

Advent is a thrilling declaration that God speaks to people. God speaks to you. God speaks to me. At the fullness of time, in Jesus, the Word made flesh, God spoke to us all.

THE PRAYER

Lord Jesus, you are the Word of God among us. We choose to hear you, to obey you, to follow you, and to be led by you into greater wholeness and awareness of your love for us this Advent. In Jesus' name, amen.

THE QUESTION

- What could you do to spend more time in the Gospels this Advent season, taking in the stories of Jesus, discovering (or rediscovering) how the Father wants to speak to you through the life of Christ?

12

JESUS IS THE LIGHT OF THE WORLD

JOHN 8:12

When Jesus spoke again to the people, he said, "I am the light of the world. Whoever follows me will never walk in darkness, but will have the light of life."

CONSIDER THIS

A third, important Advent image that feeds the roots of Jesus' story is the image of God as *light*. Light is part of the biblical narrative from the very beginning of time. In the storyline of Jesus, we discover that God is always bringing light into dark places, clarity and truth into the dim shadows of a broken world. In Advent, Jesus comes to us as the Light of the World.

Jesus is the light that dispels the shadows that lurk in the human heart. From the garden to the Gospels, from the Great Commission to the great city of the New Jerusalem, God has been, is, and will be lighting up hearts, and lighting up the world.

There is a high probability that for those of us who put up Christmas lights in or around our home, one of our favorite things to do is to turn off all the other lights in order to see them glow.

Maybe you do what my family does; during the Christmas season we take drives around different neighborhoods in our town to see the hard work people have invested in decorating their houses with way too many lights.

Some well-known homes in our town are so lit up they can be seen from a few streets over, and probably from space. These domestic spectacles even have a radio station signal you can tune in to in your car to see their lights dance along with the music.

The point is this. Light is best seen, maybe even best understood for its value and power, when it shines in the dark.

"And God said, 'Let there be light,' and there was light" (Gen. 1:3). The darkness of the chaotic and meaningless void was lit up by the Lord of creation. The Gospel of John picks up this theme and says that God's very being is light: "This is the message we have heard from him and declare to you: God is light; in him there is no darkness at all" (1 John 1:5). Revelation ties a bow on the image by saying about Christ in the New Jerusalem: "The city does not need the sun or the moon to shine on it, for the glory of God gives it light, and the Lamb is its lamp" (Rev. 21:23).

In the Old Testament, the people of God were called to be a light, shining the truths of the nature of God, the ways of worship, and how to treat one another, into the world. "I will also make you a light for the Gentiles, that my salvation may reach to the ends of the earth" (Isa. 49:6).

When Jesus comes on to the scene, he declares: "I am the light of the world. Whoever follows me will never walk in darkness, but will have the light of life" (John 8:12). John spends a considerable amount of time reinforcing the image for us: "The true light that gives light to everyone was coming into the world" (John 1:9). "The light shines in the darkness, and the darkness has not overcome it" (John 1:5). "Yet I am writing you a new command; its truth is seen in him and in you, because the darkness is passing and the true light is already shining" (1 John 2:8).

Jesus turns to us and says: "You are the light of the world" (Matt. 5:14). We are to shine like stars in the sky (Phil. 2:15), living as children of light in our families, towns, and cities: "For you were once darkness, but now you are light in the Lord. Live as children of light" (Eph. 5:8). "Let your light so shine before men, that they may see your good works and glorify your Father in heaven" (Matt. 5:16).

You and I are lights in the world, following the Light of the World. Step into the darkness into which Christ walks with you, bearing the good news of Jesus' love for all you meet, and shine like a star in our generation.

THE PRAYER

Light of the World, shine your love on our hearts this season. We know there are dark places for you to reveal, to bring your loving light to, so that we can be set free from those things that are still hidden within us. Let us shine the light of your love to everyone who meets us in this season. In Jesus' name, amen.

THE QUESTIONS

- What environments have you been called to be a light within, in your home, church, or city?

- How could you be an even brighter light in those environments this Advent season?

13

JESUS IS A FRIEND OF SINNERS

JOSHUA 2:17–18, 21

Now the men had said to her [Rahab], "This oath you made us swear will not be binding on us unless, when we enter the land, you have tied this scarlet cord in the window through which you let us down, and unless you have brought your father and mother, your brothers and all your family into your house. . . ."

"Agreed," she replied. "Let it be as you say."

So she sent them away, and they departed. And she tied the scarlet cord in the window.

CONSIDER THIS

As we turn again to the genealogy of Jesus in our study of his faith and family roots this Advent, a fascinating woman is named in Matthew 1 as part of his lineage—Rahab. Her faith that God had favored the people of Israel, a faith expressed in her hiding of the Hebrew spies who were assessing the land and Jericho's weaknesses, became the hallmark of how we remember her.

Rahab is an ancestor of the Lord Jesus Christ, and what makes her so unique is that it seems that her occupation was that of a prostitute.

Matthew wants to make sure we see her mentioned in Jesus' genealogy in the first chapter of his gospel. What is going on here?

When you look in the mirror, do you always see your best self? "Good morning," you say. "You are one shining example of a human being! What a joy it is to be you today, to actually *be* you. God loves you, adores you, in fact—and it's more obvious why every single day. You are the one of the best of us, friend. Now let's brush those teeth and get out there so the world can be a better place!"

If you say something like that each morning, good on you! A wise mentor once told me, "Humility is not too high a view of yourself or too low a view of yourself—it's an accurate view of yourself." If you're anything like me, however, you typically see not only the beautiful work that God has done in your life, you also see the blemishes, the mistakes, the regrets, and the struggles that even followers of Jesus still attempt to carry around in our memory long after he has set us free. You and I see our whole story staring back at us in the mirror—and we often have little grace for ourselves as we do.

Jesus, however, sees your story, knows your story, just as he knew the story of every sinner he was accused of treating as a friend (Matt. 9:10–12). When Jesus sees you and me, he never sees us according to our past, failings, or broken story only—he calls us by our name, sees us as we are to him, and he calls us beloved. We are never as far from God as we may feel like we are. A door of hope is always open with his Advent invitation welcoming us in: "Come, exchange your worst for my best."

Rahab must have had hard days considering her own past. As a prostitute, the narratives about her, uttered in the streets of the city, were most probably demeaning, belittling, and derogatory. Imagine no one caring about your story, how you got to where you are, and offering no compassion for you in your situation. Then, something miraculous happens in her life, just as it happens in ours. Rahab is given an opportunity to show faith, to take God as he is and as he comes to her, and to believe. She takes that opportunity, just as every friend of Jesus has taken that opportunity over thousands of years. Rahab becomes a friend of God with one decision of trust.

The next morning, when she looked in the mirror, is it possible that instead of seeing the same broken woman she saw every other day, that the winds of faith blowing through her spirit enabled her to catch a glimpse of the beautiful daughter of God the Father saw her to be? Faith can have that effect on a person. It often does; faith calls us out of our old story and welcomes into a new one—as the Spirit opens us to who we were made to be.

In Matthew 1:5, Rahab is mentioned in Jesus' genealogy, and in Hebrews 11:31 she is named in the "Hall of Faith": "By faith the prostitute Rahab, because she welcomed the spies, was not killed with those who were disobedient." In other words, Rahab *believed*.

Jesus, born under a Bethlehem sky all those years ago, was born to be a friend of sinners. Sinners were members of his own family, and their stories were not unfamiliar to him. As a salvation storyteller, Jesus knew how to turn a story around with a word, a touch, and a glimpse of pure love.

Jesus is a friend of sinners. You and I are called to be the same, knowing our own stories, and from where we have come by the grace and mercy of Christ. You and I are in good company with the Lord who receives us as we are, and shows us, along the way, who we are becoming by grace.

DAN WILT

Jesus, friend of sinners, we thank you for all you have done and are doing in our lives. Continue to transform us day by day until we become like you in every way. Transform our desires to match your own. Transform our thoughts to match your own. And give us eyes to see those who are broken by sin, ministering your love to them with compassion, forgiveness, and empathy. In Jesus' name, amen.

THE QUESTIONS

- In what ways, throughout your faith walk with Jesus, have you experienced him befriending you even when you were far from him?

- How could you extend that same friendship and acceptance to those not walking with God in your network of relationships?

14

JESUS STAYS WITH YOU

RUTH 1:16–17

But Ruth replied, "Don't urge me to leave you or to turn back from you. Where you go I will go, and where you stay I will stay. Your people will be my people and your God my God. Where you die I will die, and there I will be buried. May the LORD deal with me, be it ever so severely, if even death separates you and me."

CONSIDER THIS

A major theme in Advent is that Christ comes to us as Emmanuel, which means "God with us." As we move through Jesus' faith family history, drawing on stories of people who walked with God in exemplary ways, and connecting them to the life of Christ, we come to Ruth. Ruth is a model of what it means for Jesus to *stay* with us through all we experience.

A few years ago I had major reconstructive surgery on my foot. It would be months before I could walk normally again, and the physiotherapy was grueling. One day, alone in pain and feeling as if the ordeal would never end, I received a text from a dear brother in Christ. He asked if now would be a good time for him to come over. I told him I wouldn't be much company, but sure.

There in my living room, my foot propped up and my mind foggy from medication, we sat. We talked about anything and everything under the sun. There were long lulls in the conversation. If I wasn't so distracted by the pain it would have felt awkward. The lulls didn't seem to matter to him. I kept wondering when he would think it was time for him to leave. But he seemed to have nowhere else to be.

After a while, I realized what was happening. He had just come to be there, to sit with me in my struggle. He had come to stay a while, sit a spell, take a load off—with me. He had come to listen, to make me laugh, and to be a friend to me in my season of hard healing. Maybe you have a friend who has done the same for you.

Maybe you have been that friend.

The friendship and family kinship between Ruth and her mother-in-law, Naomi, is one for the history books. Ruth, a Moabite, was devoted to her Israelite mother-in-law after the death of their male family members. In Ruth 1:16–17, she says the words that forever endear her to the Jewish people: "Where you go I will go, and where you *stay* I will *stay*." Ruth *stayed*.

She eventually marries Boaz, her kinsman-redeemer (that's worth a study sometime), and becomes a part of the family line of the Incarnate Son of God, Jesus. A woman who *stays* is part of the family line of the Lord who stays—the Lord who stays with us through it all.

Stay. In John 15:4–5, Jesus says these words to his disciples: "Remain in me, as I also remain in you. . . . If you remain in me and I in you, you will bear much fruit." The Greek word for "remain," also translated "abide," is the word *meno*—put simply, it means to *stay*. In other words, stay a while. Sit a spell. Don't go anywhere. Remain—without needing to leave. He calls us to stay in him, and tells us that he will stay in, with, us. Emmanuel, *God with us.* There it is for our Advent reclaiming—Jesus is the Staying Lord.

Advent reminds us that the covenant loyalty and love God showed in history is the same covenant loyalty he shows us now in Christ. The gap between our Creator and us has been bridged by the presence of Jesus. He's not going anywhere. Neither should we.

Jesus, no matter what you are going through, is your Staying Lord. He is the present, remaining, Emmanuel, God-with-us King—and he is in no rush to leave your side. He is with you in sweet conversation, today, by his Spirit working within you. No matter where you are, in a hopeless valley of the heart, or on a mountaintop of highest praise, Jesus *stays* with you. He's here, with you—all the way.

THE PRAYER

Staying Lord, we desire to remain in you, and to have you remain in us. Our hearts are prone to wander, Jesus, as the old hymn says, but this Advent we choose to reorient ourselves to your unshakeable, unrelenting, loving presence in our lives. We take comfort in your nearness to us as we walk together through the days and weeks ahead in this Christian New Year. We're not letting go; we will stay with you just as you stay with us. In Jesus' name, amen.

THE QUESTION

- Have you ever felt the Lord staying with you, hanging in there with you, when others couldn't give you what you needed in time or attention? As you remember, bless him, praise him, thank him, for never leaving you or forsaking you (Heb. 13:5).

15

JESUS IS KING OF THE HUMAN HEART

1 SAMUEL 16:7, 12B–13A

But the LORD said to Samuel, ". . . The LORD does not look at the things people look at. People look at the outward appearance, but the LORD looks at the heart." . . .

Then the LORD said, "Rise and anoint him; this is the one."

So Samuel took the horn of oil and anointed him in the presence of his brothers, and from that day on the Spirit of the LORD came powerfully upon David.

CONSIDER THIS

"Once in royal David's city," goes the familiar Christmas carol. It reminds us of the ancient promise that through a royal family line, from the lineage of the great Hebrew King, David, the Messiah would be born. Our Advent verse returns to us: "A shoot will come up from the stump of Jesse [David's father]; from his roots a Branch will bear fruit" (Isa. 11:1). David, the son of Jesse, will be a key star in the constellation of spiritual royalty that leads to the birth of the bright Morning Star (Rev. 22:16), Jesus—the King of the human heart.

David. In 1 Samuel 16, Samuel the prophet is told by the Lord to seek out the new king chosen to lead his people, a king God would choose from among the sons of Jesse of Bethlehem. Samuel finds Jesse and evaluates each of his sons, searching for kingly qualities and a royal bearing in each young man. But the Lord God will have none of it: "Do not consider his appearance or his height," the Lord says. God knows exactly what he's looking for. While Samuel looks on the outward appearance, God is looking on the heart (1 Sam. 16:7).

David is framed in history as a man after God's own heart (1 Sam. 13:14; Acts 13:22). Why is he framed that way? He is anything but morally perfect and behaviorally sound. Power can corrupt, and David's lusts led him into adultery and the murder of an innocent man. Once again, Jesus' family tree, royal as it is, is full of the kinds of real people whose stories should make us all grateful that the Lord of abundant grace accepts and works with us just as we are.

What attributes did David show that made him so noteworthy as a man whose heart was after God's own? David was a worshipper at heart. His focus on intimate praise and the acclaim of his Father in heaven fills the book of Psalms, which in turn has filled the hearts of worshippers for millennia. David knew he was loved. David also knew how to repent when he had sinned, even in his most hard-hearted moments. He understood that without the favor and presence of God he was nothing. David was humble in this respect, and though he did a few glaringly wrong things in his lifetime, he could receive correction. David was a man who sought to obey God over the trajectory of his lifetime, and this kept him tethered to the heart of God toward him, and the will of God being done through him.

The Lord is never after perfection; our journey will always be uneven at best. He is after the heart. And like David, he uses the small, foolish things of this world, those people that break the "how a leader should look" rules and lead from a heart devoted to God, to confound the wise in this world's eyes (1 Cor. 1:27). When Jesus comes on the scene, he comes as an infant—with the heart of a King. Who would have thought that an infant would make great kings tremble; that a child would shake the very foundations of hell? When the hands are moved by a heart after God, there is no end to what God can accomplish through us.

From the root of David's heart will come a branch, and that branch will be known as Jesus, the Messiah, the King of the human heart.

THE PRAYER

King of the human heart, we stand in awe of your great love, a love that is changing us from the inside out, taking us from glory to glory as each day passes. Your wisdom is guiding us, your love is transforming us, and your patience is pacing us along this journey of faith. This Advent, we say, once again, that there is no one in heaven or on earth that we desire more than you (Ps. 73:25). Give us a heart like David, like Jesus—that pursues your glory above all else. In Jesus' name, amen.

THE QUESTIONS

- Have you ever looked at the outward appearance of others, comparing yourself to them and falling short of your own inward expectations of yourself?

- If God looks on the heart, instead of on the outward appearance, what is he seeing in your heart right now?

16

JESUS IS THE LEADER GIVEN TO US

ISAIAH 9:6–7

For to us a child is born, to us a son is given, and the government will be on his shoulders. And he will be called Wonderful Counselor, Mighty God, Everlasting Father, Prince of Peace. Of the greatness of his government and peace there will be no end. He will reign on David's throne and over his kingdom, establishing and upholding it with justice and righteousness from that time on and forever. The zeal of the LORD Almighty will accomplish this.

CONSIDER THIS

Feeding the roots of Jesus' family story are prophecies, this one delivered to and by the prophet Isaiah, who lived roughly seven hundred years before the birth of Christ. This Advent prophecy, beginning with the words, "For to us a child is born, to us a son is given," is brought out into the light every year as the Christian New Year begins.

While the world searches adamantly for gifted leaders to guide us, with their promises of a prosperous nation and a kinder society, Jesus was given as a gift to us from a source beyond us—our Creator. The one who made us knows the exact kind of leader we need.

Jesus was given to us, from the Father, for humanity and our condition, to lead each one of us from spiritual imprisonment to the freedom of the new creation life. Jesus leads us from simply living to a life of awakening.

Jesus was given to us, from the Father, to model for us a mode of kingdom leadership that puts the Father's ends and goals first—a remarkable form of leadership that springs from an unwavering, transcendent perspective on what is best for us all. Learned through intimacy with the Father, Jesus speaks what the Father speaks and does what the Father does in full view of us all (John 5:19; 12:49).

Jesus was given to us, from the Father, to establish a kingdom that would inhabit the human heart rather than a geopolitical location, an establishing of an inward reign by which a person is truly and utterly changed, and through which a renewed humanity would lead others to wholeness, to belovedness, and to the true *shalom* (peace) of God. Nations are collections of individuals, and Jesus pursued the individual knowing that changing the heart of one leads to changing the hearts of the many. The eternal government, the providential politics of Jesus, will always transcend the human structures so exposed and humbled by time.

Jesus was given to us, from the Father, in the form of a child. Innocence, growth, maturity, and dependence are integral to his story, as they are integral to our own. In other words, he came *like* us, in every respect, that he might lead us into the fullness of being a child of God (Heb. 2:17).

Jesus was given to us, from the Father, named by names that characterize his divine-human life unveiled before us (John 1:9–13). He is called *Wonderful*. Amazing. Breathtaking. Beyond understanding. He is called *Counselor*. Guide. Educator. Encourager. He is called *Mighty God*. Strong. Immovable. Unchanging. He is called the *Everlasting Father*. Son of the Most High. One being with the Father (John 10:30; the Nicene Creed). He is called the *Prince of Peace*. Chief Executive Officer, Chief Operations Officer, and Chief Creative Officer of Shalom—the all-pervasive peace of God.

Leadership is what the world needs from a Messiah—leadership that is motivated by pure, divine love and that is faithfully guiding us to the new creation ahead.

Be assured of this: Jesus will rule and reign over the kingdoms of this world, and they will become the kingdoms of our Lord and of his Christ (Rev. 11:15). The Lord's passion, the Lord's energetic purpose, will make it so. Let it be, Lord; let it be.

THE PRAYER

Jesus, you come to us in a time when the ways and politics of humankind have failed us as much as they have served us. You choose the human heart to reign within, and we yield ours once again in this passage through Advent. Let our allegiance to you and your lordship rule over all other loyalties in my life. In Jesus' name, amen.

THE QUESTIONS

- In the past years, have you had any allegiances or loyalties that you felt ruled over your inward commitment to Christ from time to time? What were they, and how can you get back on track?

17

JESUS IS IMMANUEL, GOD WITH US

ISAIAH 7:14

Therefore the Lord himself will give you a sign: The virgin will
conceive and give birth to a son, and will call him Immanuel.

CONSIDER THIS

Another Advent prophecy that feeds the roots of the family story
of Christ is one that speaks into Christ's coming to us in his first
advent, and reflects into Christ returning to us in his second
advent (or second coming). It is found in Isaiah 7:14 and carries
the freight of the entire Christmas story in one, single sentence:
*Therefore the Lord himself will give you a sign: The virgin will conceive
and give birth to a son, and will call him Immanuel.*

The Lord himself is going to give a sign, according to the prophet,
and that sign will be threefold in its clarity and provision: 1) a
virgin will give birth, 2) the child will be a son, and 3) the child will
be given the name "Immanuel."

First, the Lord is God of the *unexpected process*. A virgin will have
a child. That sentence doesn't sound normal in any way. In other
words, how we think a thing should happen, isn't always the way

(if ever) the Lord thinks it should happen. "'For my thoughts are not your thoughts, neither are your ways my ways,' declares the LORD. 'As the heavens are higher than the earth, so are my ways higher than your ways and my thoughts than your thoughts'" (Isa. 55:8–9).

Second, the Lord is God of the *human process*. The child born will be a son. Unlike the sentence before it, that sentence actually sounds *too* normal. We seem to need more spiritual confetti and fireworks to confirm that God is present than God desires to give. Yes, there were many wonders that surrounded the birth of Jesus, but we have no indication that Jesus' birth, in the stable with Mary and Joseph, was anything other than normal. A woman gave birth to a son. This is the Lord's grand entrance, and sets the stage for the combined normalcy, and miraculous quality, of Jesus' life among us.

Third, the Lord is God of the *relational process*. The child will be called *Immanuel*. In other words, there will be no distance between the covenant-making God and his beloved people. Jesus will say hello, will share meals, will walk and talk with us as anyone else would. But his name, and the meaning behind it, will make the relationships different than any other we could imagine.

Jesus' name is Y'shua, or Joshua, which was a common Jewish boy's name at the time. It means, "the Lord saves." Yet Jesus' name is infused by a powerful name unused by anyone else in the Scriptures—the name, Immanuel, "God with us."[3] When Matthew uses the name in 1:23, he translates it for the reader to confirm the connection between the naming of Jesus and the naming prophecy in Isaiah 7. Then, at the end of his gospel, in 28:20, he confirms that Jesus, Immanuel, will be "with us" until the end of the ages.

---

3. For more on this, I commend N. T. Wright's *Matthew for Everyone, Part 1* (Westminster: John Knox Press, 2004).

The Father is whispering his agenda into the world by the very process we will see unfolding in Jesus' birth. The Lord will be present with us, coming to us by an unexpected process, a very human process, and a very relational process. Here is the Advent God of the inconceivable, the conceivable, and the communal—the surprise, the normal, and the near.

In Immanuel, the Father is present to us, and says "Here I am." In response, we say, "Here I am." "Here I am" is one of the most powerful phrases that can be prayed by a human being; to be present to God, to be utterly attentive and wholly available, is the goal of the Christian life.

In Jesus, the great I Am says to you, to me: "Here, I am."

THE PRAYER

Immanuel, we are entering a day where knowing you are with us is as important as it will ever be. Here we are to respond to your "Here I am"; lead us in your ways as we encourage others to experience the nearness of your presence. In Jesus' name, amen.

THE QUESTIONS

- In what situations do you most sense the Lord's name—Immanuel, God with us—being true to your relationship with him? In worship? In prayer?

- In this Christian New Year, how can you cultivate being present to Jesus as he is present to you?

18

JESUS ENTERS THE WORLD THROUGH THE SMALL

MICAH 5:2

"But you, Bethlehem Ephrathah, though you are small among the clans of Judah, out of you will come for me one who will be ruler over Israel, whose origins are from of old, from ancient times."

MATTHEW 2:4–6

When he had called together all the people's chief priests and teachers of the law, he asked them where the Messiah was to be born. "In Bethlehem in Judea," they replied, "for this is what the prophet has written: "'But you, Bethlehem, in the land of Judah, are by no means least among the rulers of Judah; for out of you will come a ruler who will shepherd my people Israel.'"

CONSIDER THIS

Jesus came to us not only from a people and a story; he also came to us in a place: Bethlehem, in Israel.

Big cities hold great appeal to the modern mind. The lights, the activity, the opportunities, the options, and even the anonymity provide a draw to those wanting to experience the very best that life has to offer. In a city, you can get known. In a city, you can get whatever you want, whenever you want it. In a city, you can hide away, and perhaps no one will come knocking on your door because it takes too long to get there.

But for we who grew up in small towns, we had a different experience. The lights are quaint down at the hardware store, especially at Christmas and when the "A" in the neon sign is flickering. The activities are, well, limited. The opportunities are endless, *if* you know someone at one of the three businesses offering a job. The options are interesting for dining; in my town there was the pizza place and the breakfast place and a few other almost-out-of-business spots, and then the diner if you were in the mood for less gourmet cuisine. And as for anonymity, it's pretty hard to escape the fact that literally everyone in your town probably knows where you live, and could guide someone to your house without even looking up your address.

Bethlehem seems to have been the latter. At the time of Jesus' birth, the population may have been one thousand or less (some estimates say three hundred or less). Bethlehem is the birthplace of David, the son of Jesse the Bethlehemite (1 Sam. 16:1), the root from which Jesus comes to us. The name "Bethlehem," in Hebrew, means the "House of Bread." Beautiful. The Bread of Life comes into the world, in a small village named the "House of Bread" on the outskirts of Jerusalem. How fitting. A small town feeds the world, like the loaves of bread in Jesus' hands fed the masses.

In my university years, I studied for a season at an institute on a hill near Bethlehem in Israel. Through a strange series of circumstances, after taking a bus across the country to ask for my wife's hand in marriage (it's a long story), I ended up being lost outside of Bethlehem at 2 a.m. I had gotten off the bus at the wrong stop, and there were no more buses to be found. When I was finally pointed in the direction of the school where I was staying, I had to run across a field to get home. For a moment, I paused, looked up at the stars, and thought, *Jesus was born here*. My eyes welled up, and I continued running to my destination.

From the small places, the out of the way places, the places where one wonders if anything good can come out of them, comes God's greatest deliverance of all. "Though you are small," little town, "out of you will come a ruler, who will shepherd my people Israel" (Mic. 5:2; Matt. 2:6).

Do you ever feel small, hidden, out of the way or misunderstood? If so, count it all joy. The Lord loves to come to, and work through, the small.

THE PRAYER

Jesus, you entered the world through the small. It's from the small places, where our best intentions crash into our daily struggle, that your glory radiates. You know how small we can feel at times, how insignificant our day-to-day lives can feel in the scope of eternity. But it is in the small things you work, and we know you will work through us. In Jesus' name, amen.

THE QUESTIONS

- Are there small things you are doing right now that the Lord has led you to do, but you are wondering if they are significant?

- In light of today's daily text, how might you see them in a different light?

19

JESUS INVOLVES FAMILY IN THE ADVENT PROJECT

LUKE 1:11–13, 16–17

Then an angel of the Lord appeared to him, standing at the right side of the altar of incense. When Zechariah saw him, he was startled and was gripped with fear. But the angel said to him: "Do not be afraid, Zechariah; your prayer has been heard. Your wife Elizabeth will bear you a son, and you are to call him John. . . . He will bring back many of the people of Israel to the Lord their God. And he will go on before the Lord, in the spirit and power of Elijah, to turn the hearts of the parents to their children and the disobedient to the wisdom of the righteous—to make ready a people prepared for the Lord."

CONSIDER THIS

Advent is a time for families. And it is through families—the family of God and faithful natural families—that God works.

In the beginning of our Advent journey exploring the roots of Jesus, we considered that we each come from someone (family lines), somewhere (locations), and something (stories). When we meet Jesus, and we join him on the path to the awakened life, there is a connecting of threads that goes on, often unseen, in the background.

We become a part of the family of God, a fellowship of like-minded and like-hearted believers whose goal and aim is to glorify God in the time we are given on earth. We are swept up into a plan for the world that is so much greater than our own, and is better than any adventure we could dream up for ourselves.

Elizabeth and Zechariah were swept up into the Advent story, after spending most of their lives going about their normal day-to-day as a Hebrew family. A Levitical priest, Zechariah, encounters an angel while at the altar of incense in the temple. His wife, Elizabeth, a relative of Mary, is about to become pregnant with John (the Baptist), who will "go on before the Lord, in the spirit and power of Elijah . . . to make ready a people prepared for the Lord" (Luke 1:17).

With the nation of Israel under the thumb of the Romans, the idea that their son was about to be used by God to shake up both the faithful and the faithless to awaken to God was most probably a wonderful prospect. Some parents want their children to grow up to be contributing members of society. Elizabeth and Zechariah were probably quite happy to raise a son whose zeal for the Lord would press the buttons of the unruly hearts of their people.

When Jesus opens a heart to receive him, and to embrace the fullness of the gospel, his intent is never to stop there. He plans to use anyone in one's natural family who will come along, and, if not, the family of God given to us to encourage us in our faith. There is always a network of those impacted, who get swept up in what the Lord is doing in our midst.

The Advent project was an extended family affair from the beginning, and is intended to be so with us as well. Jesus involves families in the holy work of welcoming of Jesus into their hearts, homes, churches, and cities. Families become intercessory cells, prayer posses, enlisted by the Holy Spirit to partner with Christ in the breaking down of strongholds: "The weapons we fight with are not the weapons of the world. On the contrary, they have divine power to demolish strongholds" (2 Cor. 10:4).

The family of God was designed to work together, just as Elizabeth and Zechariah had a significant role to play in both John and Jesus coming to maturity together, ready to face the fire that would come with their mission to bring God's love and power on earth.

John would "make ready a people prepared for the Lord" (Luke 1:17), and Jesus would fulfill the words of Luke 4:18–19: "The Spirit of the Lord is on me, because he has anointed me to proclaim good news to the poor. He has sent me to proclaim freedom for the prisoners and recovery of sight for the blind, to set the oppressed free, to proclaim the year of the Lord's favor."

Parenting the central figures of Advent was no easy task, and neither is carrying awakening in our hearts for our homes, churches, and cities. But, by the power of the Holy Spirit at work within us, he will see it accomplished.

THE PRAYER

Lord of your brave family, we surrender our own hearts to work with the family of God, and our own natural family as able, to see your kingdom come, your will be done, here on earth as it is being done in heaven. Show us the part we have to play, and lead us into acts of faith that open hearts to awakening. In Jesus' name, amen.

- How has the family of God become a community with which you can participate in sharing the love of God in your town or city?

- Is there something you have planned as a way of helping others for which you could stop and pray, right now, for God to move in awakening?

20

JESUS PREPARES THE WAY FOR US

LUKE 1:41–44

When Elizabeth heard Mary's greeting, the baby leaped in her womb, and Elizabeth was filled with the Holy Spirit. In a loud voice she exclaimed: "Blessed are you among women, and blessed is the child you will bear! But why am I so favored, that the mother of my Lord should come to me? As soon as the sound of your greeting reached my ears, the baby in my womb leaped for joy."

CONSIDER THIS

The roots of Jesus run deep into the soil of his faith-family story—and they also run side to side with those who were his contemporaries and Advent partners. For Jesus, one must consider what would have happened if his relative, John, had not been born onto the scene at the same time. As we look at the Advent, we meet John first leaping in the womb of his mother, Elizabeth, delighted from before either child was born in all that God was about to do (Luke 1:41–44).

Partnership is an essential part of Christlike living in the world. Banded discipleship points us to a way of becoming God's love to one another, and God's love to the world, that lifts us out of more functional Christian paradigms of church and invites us into an intimately relational paradigm of deep community. (For more about banded discipleship, see discipleshipbands.com.)

John was a partner with Jesus, and with the Trinity, in seeing the Advent plan of salvation through. Coming into the world a few months before Jesus, as far as we can tell from the Scriptures, John was a forerunner of Christ in many ways. He had a part to play in calling the nation to repentance, and his ministry was in full motion before Jesus began his. John the Baptist was the way maker; Jesus was the Way.

Just as John laid down his life to see Jesus fulfill his ministry, so too Jesus laid down his life to see us come into the fullness of intimacy with God that the Father so desired. We see John faithfully doing his work, even to the point of facing death, and Jesus then doing the same—moving toward a death that would mean the rescue of humanity.

In Advent, we must pause to consider how Jesus prepared the way for you and I to come to know him as the Way that leads to life (Ps. 16:11). The Incarnation is a celebration of intervention, of the day when the Father gave his very best to see us become our very best before him. Jesus is God's very best, given to the world. He not only taught the way to the Father; he was the Way, the Truth, and the Life—and still is.

Christmas, like Easter, is not a static event. It is a dynamic interplay of God's continued work in the creation to restore it to himself, restoring his image-bearers to communion with himself and one another to attend to redemptive work. Jesus continues to make a way in you, your home, your church, and your city to come back to him from the exile of the heart we all are so easily given to.

In this, Jesus, like John, prepares a way for us to return, again and again, to our first love. Made for love, Jesus is the Way to its full, and unending experience for you, for me, and for those in your community.

THE PRAYER

Jesus, the Way, you continually invite me to follow paths that lead to you, to wholeness, and to community, ultimately leading to the Father's heart. If you don't cease your constant welcoming of us, we won't cease our continual return when we wander. We choose you, the Way that leads to life; make us a way-maker for those who are yet to return, by your Spirit. In Jesus' name, amen.

THE QUESTIONS

- Do you know of someone who needs some help right now to find their way to, or back to, Christ?

- What one thing could you do to help remove the barriers they believe are between them and God, to support the Spirit's process of wooing them home?

21

JESUS IS RAISED BY THE FAITHFUL

LUKE 1:26–28

In the sixth month of Elizabeth's pregnancy, God sent the angel
Gabriel to Nazareth, a town in Galilee, to a virgin pledged to
be married to a man named Joseph, a descendant of David.
The virgin's name was Mary. The angel went to her and said,
"Greetings, you who are highly favored! The Lord is with you."

MATTHEW 1:18–20A

This is how the birth of Jesus the Messiah came about: His mother Mary
was pledged to be married to Joseph, but before they came together,
she was found to be pregnant through the Holy Spirit. Because Joseph
her husband was faithful to the law, and yet did not want to expose her
to public disgrace, he had in mind to divorce her quietly. But after he had
considered this, an angel of the Lord appeared to him in a dream . . .

CONSIDER THIS

As Advent begins to flow into Christmas, the Christian New Year
takes us to the heights of celebration as we remember the birth of
Jesus. We call this the Incarnation, the God we worship becoming
flesh and blood, like one of us in every respect (Heb. 2:17). Advent
and Christmas are part of what we call the Cycle of Light, made up

of Advent (anticipation), Christmas (celebration), and Epiphany (proclamation).

In the Cycle of Light, we see Christ's radiance shining in the eyes of Mary and Joseph. Each of these two amazing souls shares a story in the Gospels, and each has their own history they brought to the moment. God does not hit "delete" on our past when it comes to a moment he desires to use us in a special way. Who we have become, over the years, formed by our responses to our challenges, limitations, influences, and family lives, all comes to bear on that moment.

The Lord sees faithfulness in our stories, forged in private moments when we could have turned away, turned back, or turned off when he wanted to work in and through us in the little things. Luke 16:10 says it clearly: "Whoever can be trusted with very little can also be trusted with much, and whoever is dishonest with very little will also be dishonest with much." Our faithfulness in the little things will always mean more to God than we may be aware of in the moment. He sees what no one else does. He knows what truly motivated us, moved us, evidenced by how we handled the unseen and seemingly insignificant times of obedience.

And that brings us to Mary. Luke 1:26–28 simply notes that Mary is "highly favored." It's possible we could read right over that statement and miss its import. Mary has *favor* with God. If you have favor with God, you don't need it with anyone else. Mary was living a life, unseen to us and unrecorded by history, that pleased God. Mary, as far as we can tell, had been living a faithful life up to the point the angel graces her room—a life faithful to the Father, his purposes, and his values.

Joseph seems to have been the same. In Matthew 1:18–20a, we get a brief glimpse into his character, seeing that he is faithful to the law, and in this case, we can read that as a metaphor suggesting that Joseph cares what God thinks about things. When he hears of Mary's pregnancy, he wants to do his beloved betrothed no harm, choosing to keep her story out of the public eye and to end their relationship quietly. We have no indication that Joseph was anything other than eager and willing to support Mary and to raise Jesus as his own when the angel appears to him in a dream.

Faithfulness in our past gives momentum to faithfulness in our present. Faithful in little, faithful in much. That is the way the Advent story unfolds, and ours as well. Today you and I have the opportunity to trade our fear for Christ's courage, our apprehension for Christ's revelation.

And if we will be faithful in little, we will be invited to partner with Christ and other faithful people in the awakening of the world—whether that world be in the home of the neighbor next door, or in the halls of kings and queens.

THE PRAYER

Jesus, Son of God, son of Mary and Joseph, you were raised by faithful people whose lives were as simple and complex as my own. When you called them, you had already found them to be faithful friends of God, and we want to be seen as the same. This Advent teach us to be faithful in little; let our hearts move from disdain for the details to which we must attend, to delight in partnering with you in the smallest, most hidden ways. In Jesus' name, amen.

- In what little ways, public or hidden, do you believe you are partnering with God right now?

- What areas of faithfulness are you struggling with, and could you give those areas up to Jesus in surrender now? He wants to use you, and you are in training in the little things.

22

JESUS IS LORD OF THE ABSOLUTELY TERRIFIED

LUKE 2:8–12

And there were shepherds living out in the fields nearby, keeping watch over their flocks at night. An angel of the Lord appeared to them, and the glory of the Lord shone around them, and they were terrified. But the angel said to them, "Do not be afraid. I bring you good news that will cause great joy for all the people. Today in the town of David a Savior has been born to you; he is the Messiah, the Lord. This will be a sign to you: You will find a baby wrapped in cloths and lying in a manger."

CONSIDER THIS

Our Advent journey brings us to the shepherds, part of the same faith-family story as Jesus, remembered for their wonder that starry night—but also, for their sheer terror. How do you want to be remembered? Would you prefer the words "joyful" and "courageous" to come up in conversations when you are mentioned, or would you prefer the words "terrified" and "afraid" to be the character traits discussed?

Unfortunately, the shepherds didn't get to choose! These Advent heroes were terrified, and all of history since knows it. But they were terrified for a good reason—God was on the move. We do them honor when we recognize that though they were clearly shocked when the angels greeted them in the night sky, they were terrified because of the awesomeness of the cosmic drama unfolding before them. We would most probably have been just as terrified, as afraid as they were, if we had been there. The shepherds took their place within the most profound moment of human history that night, and quickly became "incarnation evangelists" telling others about what they had seen (vv. 17–18).

If you're like me, there are times in our journey of faith when we are plain, raw, straight-up scared. Can I get a witness? Life throws us a curveball, and before we can say, "Greater is he that is in me!" we've taken a hit across the bow and our battleship is sinking.

In *A Charlie Brown Christmas*, which my family watches every year at this time, Linus reads the Christmas story from Luke 2 in the King James Version. Who can forget his recitation, security blanket in hand, on that spotlit stage? Coming to verse 9, Linus says, "The glory of the Lord shone round about them, and they were *sore* afraid." *Sore* afraid. I like that phrase. Yes, "sore" means "very" in this case, but there is a playful double-meaning here. Have you ever been so afraid you were *sore*, inside and outside? I have. Your heart aches, your stomach churns, and you aren't sure that God will come through—that his words to you are believable. Linus, bearing his security blanket, because everyone needs a little support every now and again, confidently reads the Christmas story in that little spotlight on that animated stage. And if he can show some faith, so can we.

It's in those times, those times of challenge, that we can remember the shepherds—and take heart. Their fear was based in awe, in an overwhelming sense that God was active in bringing good news to his people. Sure, the situation may have felt intuitively "good" in some way, so they could assume God was at work. But terror is terror, and when we are overwhelmed and scared by a circumstance, we can learn to reinterpret it as a time for awe in what the Lord is doing and will do.

Philippians 4:6–7 says that we are to be anxious about nothing, and the spirit of command in those words cannot be missed. But neither can the tone of compassion. The writer knows that we need peace in our shock-and-awe moments, and suggests that peace lies on the other side of prayer and drawing close to the Father.

The next time you are absolutely terrified, know that the Lord is with you and is about something in the background that will not derail the plans he has for you, plans to prosper you, and to give you a hope and a future (Jer. 29:11). Lean into him in prayer, in worship, in thanks, in community with others—and stay in that place until your fear is absorbed into the presence of God.

THE PRAYER

Lord of the Terrified, thank you for being our Lord. We've known what it means to be afraid and to have you meet us in that place. Protect our hearts from getting lost in my worst expectations, and create in us, by your Spirit within, hearts that expect your highest and best as you walk with us through the challenges ahead. In Jesus' name, amen.

THE QUESTIONS

- Can you think of a moment this past year when you were terrified or afraid, and felt beside yourself in worry? How did the Lord meet you in that time, and what is your testimony on the other side?

DAN WILT

23

JESUS IS THE THEME OF MARY'S SONG

LUKE 1:46–55

And Mary said: "My soul glorifies the Lord and my spirit rejoices in God my Savior, for he has been mindful of the humble state of his servant. From now on all generations will call me blessed, for the Mighty One has done great things for me—holy is his name. His mercy extends to those who fear him, from generation to generation. He has performed mighty deeds with his arm; he has scattered those who are proud in their inmost thoughts. He has brought down rulers from their thrones but has lifted up the humble. He has filled the hungry with good things but has sent the rich away empty. He has helped his servant Israel, remembering to be merciful to Abraham and his descendants forever, just as he promised our ancestors."

CONSIDER THIS

Advent is a season of descent toward the humble stable, where a new family is born at the birth of the King of kings and Lord of lords—pointing to our larger family that transcends time and space as the people of the Covenant-Keeping God, the Lord who keeps his promises "to a thousand generations" (Ps. 105:8).

Before the moment of Jesus' birth, after Mary receives word from the angel that she is with child by the Holy Spirit, and after seeing her cousin Elizabeth, she is filled with a song of vibrant worship.

We call that song, "The Magnificat" (Latin for "my soul magnifies"). Advent is a time for worship—worship that is wild with praise, rich with memory, and packed with joy. This Advent season of descent, as the Lord of Hosts manifests his love on earth in the person of Jesus, we would do well to recount some of the lyrics of Mary's powerful song of worship.

"My soul glorifies the Lord and my spirit rejoices in God my Savior." Mary is informing her spirit, her mind, and anyone who will listen, what the activity is going on within her. She is in a state of utter and complete rejoicing in what God has done, and is about to do. We should glorify the Lord with her!

"From now on all generations will call me blessed." Mary is aware that the circumstances of today will have implications for the future. She is privileged to take on any mockery for this unique birth story. Mary knows the faithful will call her blessed. We can know that no matter what the world says, the faithful will call us blessed!

"His mercy extends to those who fear him, from generation to generation." Mary is present to the fact that what happens in one generation has implications for the next. We, too, can know that our sowing today will reap a harvest we may never see, and in this we can both trust and celebrate!

"He has performed mighty deeds with his arm; he has scattered those who are proud in their inmost thoughts." Mary knows that the humble heart is humble in one's inmost thoughts, and not just in one's demeanor. We can ask the Lord of Hosts to make us humble in our inmost thoughts, like Christ!

"He has brought down rulers from their thrones but has lifted up the humble." Mary saw the end in mind. The kingdoms of this world are becoming the kingdoms of our Lord and of his Christ (Rev. 11:15). We can, and must, see where this is all going; faith is

the assurance of things hoped for, the conviction of things not yet seen (Heb. 11:1)!

"He has filled the hungry with good things but has sent the rich away empty." Mary knew her son would be the source of food and drink (John 4:10) for humanity; and she knew the already-satisfied would choose lesser sustenance. We can bring our hunger, our thirst, to Jesus—and be filled!

"He has helped his servant Israel, remembering to be merciful to Abraham and his descendants forever, just as he promised our ancestors." Mary knew the covenant story of Israel was being fulfilled in the life of her son, Jesus; she felt the mercy of God in play for her people through the Incarnation. We can see ourselves in that long, covenant relationship that reaches deep into the roots of the story of Israel.

With Mary, let's magnify the Lord together this Advent and Christmas season!

THE PRAYER

Our souls magnify you, Lord, and our spirits rejoice in you, our Savior! In Jesus' name, amen.

THE QUESTION

- If you were writing a song of worship right now, what words to describe the Lord would you choose, and why?

24

CHRISTMAS EVE: JESUS IS ADVENT'S GREAT HIGH PRIEST

1 TIMOTHY 2:5–6

For there is one God and one mediator between God and mankind, the man Christ Jesus, who gave himself as a ransom for all people. This has now been witnessed to at the proper time.

HEBREWS 4:14–16

Therefore, since we have a great high priest who has ascended into heaven, Jesus the Son of God, let us hold firmly to the faith we profess. For we do not have a high priest who is unable to empathize with our weaknesses, but we have one who has been tempted in every way, just as we are—yet he did not sin. Let us then approach God's throne of grace with confidence, so that we may receive mercy and find grace to help us in our time of need.

CONSIDER THIS

In Advent and on this Christmas Eve, we celebrate the birth of Jesus as the King of all kings. But we must also pause to realize that in accord with the deep roots of his family story, Christ was born to us in another role as well—one that reaches back all the way to David, Jesse's son. Born in the City of David, Bethlehem, we received not only the King of the World—we also received the Great High Priest of humanity (Heb. 4:14).

On that night so long ago, Jesus was born to be our Great High Priest, to mediate between us and the Father. As part of a long line of royal priest-kings, like his ancestor, David, Jesus reminded humanity of its highest identity as the beloved of God. As we descend into the nativity narrative of the Christmas story, we descend into the moment God is born into the world "like us" (Heb. 2:17).

In other words, he knows who we are, how we are, and why we are, because he is truly one of us. Because he became one of us, living his life from infancy to adulthood, we know that he can "empathize with our weakness" as he becomes the doorway to the Father (John 14:6). Biblically, the most important role of a priest was not to lord that role over others, but rather to show others how to become a place where heaven and earth meet. Our Great High Priest came to show us the way to the fullness of our human vocation as people in whom heaven and earth meet.

Jesus is the Son of Man and the Son of God, and we understand his nature to be fully God and fully human. As followers of Jesus, we, too, can understand ourselves to be of earth and of heaven, expressions of the Father's heart carrying the Spirit of the Great High Priest within us. A priest *mediates for others*. A priest *serves before God in worship*. A priest *teaches and reminds* human beings where their dignity truly lies and in whom their identity is truly found.

Christ came to us in the Incarnation, as our Great Mediator, to show us how to be a bridge for others, pointing them to him, the way to the Father, and to build bridges for people who struggle to walk toward God over the great chasms they face. The infant Jesus bridged the gap; so, too, we can bridge a gap for those to whom the Father sends to us.

Christ came to us in the Incarnation, to show us how to serve before God in worship. You and I were not just meant to lead people in worship, as if the end goal of worship was the community. The priests ministered to the Lord himself, acclaiming him in public and in private because of their intimate communion with him.

Worship is where we learn to hear God's voice, to perceive his movements, and to love his ways. Worship that has lost this central focus on ministering to the Lord, has lost its power. As a royal priest, we spend our lives, including our days, hours, and minutes, in the presence of the Lord—thanking him, blessing him, and praising him for who he is. Ministering to the Father is a ministry Jesus came to show us.

Christ came to us in the Incarnation, to show us the way to teach others of their dignity and the dignity of other human beings, and to affirm each person's unique identity as the beloved of God. Jesus took three decades to grow into the fullness of his ministry, he used the power of modeling, of story, of parables, and of compassionate instruction to help people find their way in a dignity-degrading, identity-confusing world. As Spirit-filled and guided royal priests ourselves, we have the mandate to teach and instruct, by all means possible, those who have lost their why and their way.

Jesus, the Lord of Advent, comes to us as the Great High Priest. And we, like him, are called to the ministry of healing in the world as he leads us and teaches us his way.

THE PRAYER

Jesus, our Great High Priest, this Advent we worship you for coming to us as our living reminder of what it means to be human—and to rehumanize others. We take up the calling to be one of the royal priests of the royal priesthood

DAN WILT

(1 Peter 2:9), and to take our place as one who bridges the gaps for those far from God in my home, family, church, and city. In Jesus' name, amen.

THE QUESTIONS

- This past year, how have you been a bridge for others who were losing their dignity or forgetting their belovedness to Jesus?

- How can you be a more fully engaged royal priest of God in this year ahead?

25

CHRISTMAS DAY: JESUS IS THE ROOT OF DAVID AND THE BRIGHT MORNING STAR

REVELATION 22:16

"I, Jesus, have sent my angel to give you this testimony for the churches. I am the Root and the Offspring of David, and the bright Morning Star."

CONSIDER THIS

Christmas is here, and we rejoice together in celebration! Jesus is Immanuel, God with us. Christ is the Root and Offspring of David, and the Bright Morning Star. You came to us as King, and you will come to us again as Returning King, to reign forever. Glory to God in the highest!

From the root of David you came to us, from a people, from a place, and from a story. That story leads us to today, where the Lamb of God, the King of all kings who rules supreme, forever, is celebrated and blessed as the world's one true leader (Rev. 17:14). From that root, you came to us as our

Great High Priest. There is now one mediator between God and humankind, who lives forever to stand in the gap for us (1 Tim. 2:5; Heb. 7:25).

Then, as the Bright Morning Star, you brought the Light of the New Creation to us, revealing that salvation is here for the heart ready to be made new. Christmas is a sign and a wonder that points to the fact that all things are being made new by a God who enters the old to birth the new from within. The Light enters the darkness, in order to dispel the darkness; that is the message of Christmas.

In both these images, Christ as the root of David and as the Bright Morning Star, Christmastide is revealed to mean that God incarnates to intervene—to intervene in our mess, our injustice, our idolatry, our confusion and our hatred and our self-serving, to address the problem from the inside out—in the person of Christ.

The Deliverer the Father sends came to deliver us from the same evil that threatens every human being from the heart, spreading a slow poison into all our lives—*sin*. Just when the world thought it could continue to blame someone else, something else or its ills, to continue to wage war and to destroy lives that get in our way, Jesus arrives and exposes it all as a problem of the heart—a problem shared by every man, woman, and child on the planet.

Born in the manger, from the root of David, the problem is addressed. Jesus, the King of the new creation, revealed our hearts to us, like the Morning Star revealing the new day. Jesus was born, and both lived and died, for this work of revelation and healing of the human spirit.

Then, he rose again, ascending to the Father, to become the King of kings and the Lord of lords for all eternity. There is a human being at the right hand of God, fully God and fully human, who walked among us full of grace and truth (John 1:14). He showed us the way to live (Matt. 5–7), revealed the Father (John 17:25–26), and faced death and persecution for loving us enough to be the Way, the Truth, and the Life among us (John 14:6). And then he rose again from the grave, our Immanuel, God with us, the Root and Offspring of David, the Bright Morning Star—living and reigning forever.

That root of David, the promised Messiah, the one who shines like the Bright Morning Star, cuts through the night and welcomes you and me toward the dawn. He has come to us. Joy to the world!

Merry Christmas! God, our Immanuel, is truly with you—is truly with us.

THE PRAYER

Root of David, Bright Morning Star, you light the world with your presence and you light our hearts with your love. Thank you for your Advent among us, your coming to us, to live before us, in us, and through us in the world. Your Spirit is at work, and we ask that you would reveal to us how we can best join you in that work in the days we are given. In Jesus' name, amen.

THE QUESTION

- This Christmas Day, how can you delight in the work the Lord has done in you as you go through the activities of the day? Pause now to reflect on how the Morning Star has brought light into your life this year, and trust, with expectation, that he will do the same in the next.